2.⁰⁰

Investigating Science with Rubber Bands

by Laurence B. White, Jr.

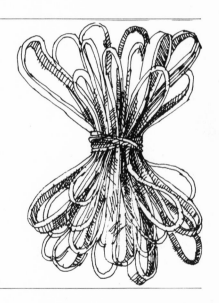

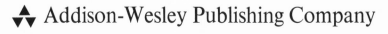

▲ Addison-Wesley Publishing Company

Reading, Massachusetts

To Norm Harris, the teacher's teacher,
who showed me the way to show you the way

Books by Laurence B. White, Jr.

Investigating Science with Coins
Investigating Science with Rubber Bands
Investigating Science with Paper
Investigating Science with Nails

**An Addisonian Press Book**

Text copyright © 1969, by Laurence B. White, Jr.
Text Philippines copyright 1969, by Laurence B. White, Jr.
Illustrations copyright © 1969, by Addison-Wesley Publishing Company, Inc.
Illustrations Philippines copyright 1969, by Addison-Wesley Publishing
Company, Inc.

All rights reserved.

The Addison-Wesley Publishing Company, Inc.

Library of Congress catalog card number 72-80505
Printed in the United States of America
Second Printing
SBN: 201-08656-5

Table of Contents

1

Rubber Band Mysteries

This is a book of adventures: not long-ago or far away episodes, but real adventures that you can have. You won't need a lot of equipment, either. With just a good supply of rubber bands and a few other things you'll be ready to start investigating mysteries as intriguing as any that ever confronted Sherlock Holmes.

Of course, you'll need something in addition to your materials, the two skills essential for any detective: observation and careful thinking. Hopefully this book will help you develop these skills; at any rate, it will certainly test your powers. To get you under way, here is a thinking mystery.

THE MYSTERY OF THE SWIMMING BAND

If you drop a rubber band in a glass of water you can prove that rubber floats—and you can use the proof to investigate a strange property of water.

A Round Band

Things Needed:
Thin rubber band
Glass or bowl of water
Bar of soap

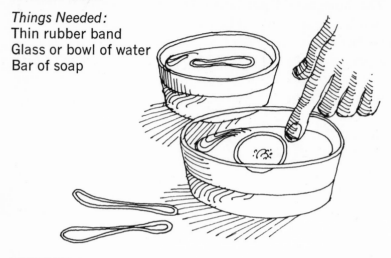

Drop the band into the water. It will float in the shape that is "built into" it. Scrape off a tiny bit of soap, and drop it carefully into the middle of the floating band. The band suddenly moves outward and forms a circle!

What is the mystery? What is happening here? Do not be in a hurry to answer the question. Why? Because most people guess wrong, and are surprised to learn what is **not** happening. The soap is not pushing the band outward into a circle.

What is happening, then? The water, outside the band, is pulling it outward.

Suppose you stretched a piece of sheet rubber tightly across the top of a glass, then took a knife and made a tiny cut in the center of the sheet. What would happen? The hole would get larger because the rubber would pull away from it. The hole gets bigger because the rubber is pulling it open wider, not because the hole is pushing outward.

The water surface is composed of a layer of water molecules that attract each other strongly. All of the molecules in the glass attract each other, but those at the surface attract one another most strongly. For this reason, the surface of the water is "tougher" than the rest of the water, almost as though it were a rubber sheet covering the water beneath it. This effect is called *surface tension*. All liquids have some degree of surface tension; water is just a good (and easily available) example.

If you float a rubber band on the water's surface, you will find that it floats very high out of the water. If you drop a bit of soap into the water, and mix it about, you will find that the band still floats, but most of it will be below the surface. Soap lowers surface tension. The band still floats because it is lighter than the water, but, without surface tension to help support it, it cannot float as high.

Soap makes a "hole" in the surface tension, just like the hole you imagined in the stretched rubber sheet. When you drop soap in the middle of the floating band, the surface tension pulls the band outward so the "hole" gets bigger.

Understanding how soap affects the surface tension of water can help you in making some rubber band boats to use in a sink or bathtub.

Rubber Band Navy

Things Needed:
Rubber bands
Scissors
Bar of soap
Bathtub or sink, with water

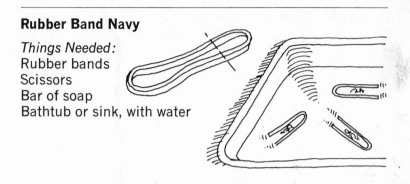

Cut the end off a rubber band to make a "U" shaped boat. Float the boat in the water, being sure that the water has no soap in it. Drop a tiny piece of soap, scraped off the bar, into the center of the boat. The boat will zoom about on the surface, powered only by its soap motor.

Here again, the boat is not being pushed forward by the soap. It is being pulled forward by the surface tension of the water, and the soap is making a hole in this tension behind, and within, the boat.

How many boats can you power at the same time? Perhaps you might try making a navy. How long will the boats continue to move? Until the holes have become large enough to cover the entire surface of the water. Then, without any surface tension, the action of the boats cannot continue. Once the action stops, you will have to let out the old water, rinse all the soap carefully away, and start again with fresh water. The larger the surface of water, the longer your navy will move about.

2

The Inside Story
of a Rubber Band

In the year 1823, in London, a coachmaker named Hancock discovered that rubber sheets could be cut into long, thin strips, and the ends of the strips then fastened together. He found these very useful, not only in his work, but for other jobs as well.

But the story of a rubber band really began further back than Hancock. More than 1000 years ago the Mayan Indians of South America found that the sap of the rubber tree, dried over a fire, had amazing and useful properties. They fashioned many articles, including the first pair of rubber shoes, from this substance.

The Mayan discovery was taken to Europe by Christopher Columbus. Three years after he had first landed in America, Columbus visited the island of Haiti, and observed the natives bouncing round balls of rubber. Delighted with this novelty, he took some of the balls back to Spain with him and presented them to Queen Isabella. Presumably the nobles of the Spanish court had as much fun with the balls as the Indian children did. But Europe was more interested in the wealth of the New World than in games, and rubber was forgotten for the next three hundred years.

Rubber didn't even get its name until the year 1770, when an experimenter discovered that a piece of the material would erase pencil marks. These first erasers were called rubbers because they could rub out marks. The name rubber stuck, and has been used ever since. But rubber's value to man was still not realized.

Fifty-three years later, in 1823, it was found that rubber could be dissolved in certain oils and sandwiched between pieces of cloth. These waterproofed pieces of cloth were then used to make raincoats. Have you ever heard of a mackintosh? Your mother might use that name for your raincoat. It was a Scotsman who first discovered how to use rubber to make waterproof cloth. His name, if you haven't already guessed, was Charles Macintosh.

At the same time that Macintosh was experimenting with waterproof cloth, Hancock, in England, was trying out the first rubber bands. In the year 1823, then, the real "star" of this book appeared.

Since then rubber has become extremely important in our daily lives. You can probably think of half-a-dozen rubber objects without even trying, from automobile tires to pencil erasers. You could really compile a long list if you tried, but more surprising than the number of items would be their short history.

Everything you use that is made of rubber ... except for rubber balls, erasers, waterproof cloth, and elastic bands ... has been invented in only the past 150 years.

RUBBER COMES FROM PLANTS

The rubber tree is one of the best known trees in the world, but few of us will ever see one. The rubber tree is called, scientifically, *Heva brasiliensis*. Like many scientific names, this one gives us some information about the plant. *Brasiliensis* looks a bit like Brazil, and that is where rubber trees were originally found. The trees are native to the Amazon Valley in South America. But, surprisingly, practically no rubber comes from South America.

In 1876 a number of young trees were brought to England and planted in the Kew Gardens in London. However, the climate was not right for them. The trees were again transplanted, this time to Ceylon, an island south of India. Here they flourished. Later, as rubber became more important, other plantations were started in the Dutch East Indies and British Malaya. Perhaps you can find Malaya, Sarawak, and North Borneo on a globe. These are all important rubber-producing areas. Singapore is called the rubber capital of the world.

The milky white sap of the rubber tree is collected by slicing the bark and allowing the juice to ooze out into a pail hung on the tree. This sap is called *latex*.

You may be able to purchase small quantities of rubber tree latex from a chemical supply house. If you can't obtain any, a similar sap can be collected from a milkweed plant, or dandelions. If you break the stems or leaves of these plants you should be able to squeeze quite a bit of the white sap into a jar. Milkweed or dandelion sap will work just like rubber tree sap for your investigations. You will need to obtain about one teaspoon of sap for the investigations in this chapter.

Make a Rubber Band

Things Needed:
Small quantity of sap

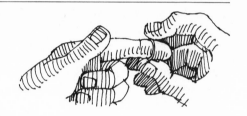

To make a rubber band coat the end of your finger with sap, down to about the first knuckle. Leave the sap on your finger for several minutes until it dries and becomes colorless. Then, gently, roll the rubber down like rolling off a stocking. When it rolls off the end, you will find that you have produced a tiny band of rubbery material. Stretch it and you will notice that it acts like a rubber band . . . but don't stretch it too far or it will break. It is not as tough as the store variety!

Why does the sap turn into this rubber-like material? Actually, it doesn't. The substance is there all the time; it is in tiny pieces which are suspended in a watery solution. On your finger, the water evaporates and the tiny pieces come together in long strands.

A Rubber Sheet

Things Needed:
Small quantity of sap
Window pane

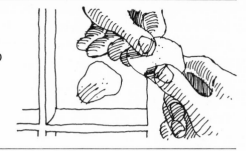

The Mayan Indians found that heat from a fire could be used to speed up the process. Heat from your finger helps in the same way.

To make a rubber sheet spread a bit of sap on a window pane. Wait until the sap dries and becomes transparent. This will take about fifteen minutes. Peel off the dried rubbery sheet very carefully.

Do not let the sides of the sheet come together or you will discover that it is very sticky, and you will not be able to separate the fold. Did the sap on the window pane dry more slowly than the sap on your finger? Did the heat of your finger speed up the drying?

Waterproofing Cloth

Things Needed:
Small quantity of sap
Small square of cloth
Glass of water

Pour a little sap on the cloth and smear it around with your finger. Set the cloth aside until it is dry. The cloth is now waterproof. If you put a few drops of water on it, you will find that the drops do not soak in.

Would this be a good, easy way to waterproof your jacket? No. You'll understand why when you conduct the Hot and Cold Cloth investigation.

Hot and Cold Cloth

Things Needed:
Waterproof cloth from last investigation
Lamp with uncovered bulb
Freezer compartment of refrigerator

Place the piece of waterproofed cloth on a light bulb for about five minutes. Be sure that the bulb is turned on, and that it is touching the cloth. When you remove the cloth you will find it is limp and sticky. This same thing might happen to your jacket if you waterproofed it with sap.

Place the cloth in the freezer of a refrigerator overnight. When you remove the cloth in the morning you will find it hard and stiff. It will stay that way for some time until it warms up. You'd be rather uncomfortable if your jacket did that on a cold winter day.

It is simple to make rubbery material from watery sap, but what you have made is very crude. Crude rubber, from the rubber tree, must still go through many processes in a rubber factory before it becomes really usable.

CRUDE RUBBER

Rubber is sent from the tree to the processing plant in any of several forms. It may be shipped as concentrated latex. This is the rubber sap, as it comes from the tree, but with a great deal of its water removed to make it much thicker. It might also be smoked over a fire to become a smoked sheet. Or it may be air-dried in the sun. Air-dried rubber is called *crepe rubber*. Still another method is to put the latex into large tanks and add acid to it. The acid causes the rubber to *coagulate* into a spongy mass. This last method makes an intriguing investigation.

Coagulating Rubber

Things Needed:
Half-teaspoon of sap
Bottle of vinegar
Glass one-fourth
  filled with water
A drinking straw

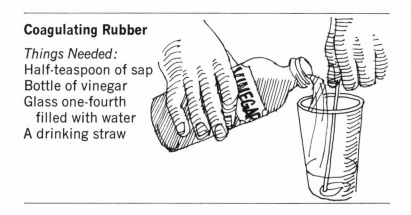

Pour about half a teaspoon of sap into the glass one-fourth filled with water. Now stir with the straw. You will find that the mixture has about the consistency of milk. Keep stirring while you pour in a little vinegar. You will feel a mass coagulating and clumping on the straw. Remove the straw and you will discover a rubbery material sticking to the end.

Vinegar is a very weak acid, called *acetic acid.* This is one of the same acids used by rubber workers to coagulate large quantities of latex.

It has been found that when rubber is prepared by heating it over a fire the process is faster if the fire is very smoky. Why? Because smoke contains an acid which helps to coagulate the latex.

Make a Rubber Ball

Things Needed:
Coagulated mass
    from last investigation

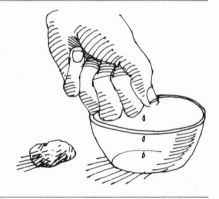

After removing the mass from the straw, hold the mass over a sink and squeeze hard. You will find that the mass is filled with little pockets of water, and there is not as much actual material as you might think at first look. Continue squeezing until most of the water is removed and you have shaped the mass into a tiny ball.

Throw the ball hard down on the floor. It will probably bounce back higher than your head. You have made a very lively ball which bounces very well. Because it is not perfectly round, it will probably bounce back and forth with an erratic action.

Curing the Ball

Things Needed:
Rubber ball from last investigation
A month of patience

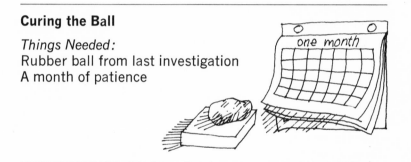

After showing the ball to your friends you might enjoy curing it. You will notice that the freshly coagulated ball is white, like the sap it was produced from. If you put it away for about a month, you will discover that it has changed. The warmth of your house, and time, will allow the remaining water to evaporate, and the chemicals in the ball will lock together better. The ball will become almost transparent, with a slight brownish color. It will be harder, and will look and feel more like the rubber in an elastic band.

The rubbery material is now somewhat cured, and on its way to being more useful. If it were commercial rubber, however, it would still have a long way to go. The rubber factory would grind it up, add other chemicals to it, bake it, and cure it again to make it still better.

Perhaps you might like to make a few of these balls for your friends. You might find another use for them, too. After they have cured, the balls are very much like the first rubbers used to erase pencil marks in 1770.

WHAT IS A RUBBER BAND?

There are many ways you might answer the question, "What is a rubber band?" You could say it is a ring of rubber. You might describe the things you can do with it.

But, to a scientist, a rubber band is a chemical: a very peculiar chemical, arranged in a particular way. Let us look, not at what a rubber band does, but, rather, at what it is.

When you consider how many different things rubber bands can do, it is surprising to learn that rubber contains just two basic elements: hydrogen and carbon. A single rubber band contains many millions of atoms, joined together in long stretchy strings. But all of the atoms are either carbon or hydrogen.

Hydrogen, by itself, is a lighter-than-air gas. It is also very flammable. You can prove its presence in a rubber band with this "sparkling" investigation. (For safety's sake, do this investigation and any others in which matches are used, in the presence of an adult.)

Hydrogen in a Rubber Band

Things Needed:
Rubber band
Metal jar cover
A match

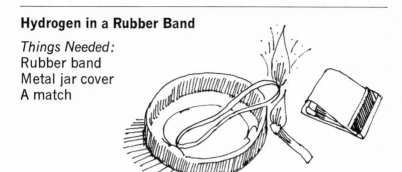

Place the rubber band in the jar cover so that one end is on the rim. Light this end with a match and observe the band as it burns. (Warning: Do not touch the band as it burns, or for several minutes afterward. Melted rubber is very hot and it will stick to your fingers.) When the rubber band burns, its flame is quite different from the flame of a match. The different flame is due to the presence of hydrogen. You will notice that it burns quickly, throws off little sparks, and produces a crackling sound. The crackling sound is actually a series of tiny explosions resulting from the rapid burning.

Carbon, the other ingredient of rubber, is found in many forms: coal, charcoal, and soot from a fire are common examples. It is also found as diamonds, in oil, and in carbon dioxide in the air. All living and once-living things contain carbon. It is not one of the most common elements in our world; but it is certainly a very important one.

Carbon in a Rubber Band

Things Needed:
Rubber band
Metal jar cover
A match
Piece of white paper

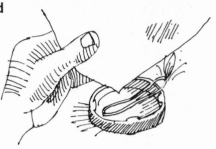

Arrange the rubber band in the jar cover as in the last investigation, and light it. While it burns, hold the paper about four inches above the flame. A black layer of soot will appear on the paper. The soot, of course, is carbon in its pure form. It is always surprising to collect such a black chemical from a light-colored rubber band.

If you rub your finger in the soot you will find that it is powdery and not at all like rubber. In the band the carbon and hydrogen atoms have been joined together in just the right way to produce molecules. Rubber molecules have qualities all their own, and are quite different from either of the atoms that make them up.

AN ELEMENT OF MYSTERY

Sulphur is another element that might be found in a rubber band. What is it doing there? Sulphur is not part of the rubber molecule; it has been added by the rubber processors, but rubber would still be rubber without it.

You can prove that sulphur is present by "coaxing" it out. To do this you must put another element near the rubber band, so that the sulphur will react with it. Some of the sulphur will leave the band and join with some of the other element. Together they will become a new chemical, quite different from either of the original elements. In this way you, as a science detective, can prove the mystery element, sulphur, is actually in the rubber band.

Cross Your Silver with Sulphur

Things Needed:
Rubber band
A quarter (dated 1964 or before)
Silver polish

Quarters made after 1964 do not contain any silver, and they won't react with the rubber band. If you can't find a suitable coin, try using a silverplated spoon or medal.

Polish the quarter and wrap the rubber band tightly around it. Dip the band-wrapped coin in water and put it aside for three days. After this time, when you remove the band, you should find some dark markings on the coin which indicate the presence of sulphur.

Silver from the coin and sulphur from the band join together very readily and form a new chemical called *silver sulphide*, which appears dark. This simple investigation is a positive test for sulphur. You can prove that rubber bands contain it . . . but, again, what is it doing there?

As soon as people discovered rubber's unusual properties, they began trying to find new uses for it. In the early 1800's dozens of experiments were made. It seemed reasonable that rubber could be used to make better clothing and boots, but there were many problems. When the weather got hot the rubber became sticky and even melted. Imagine wearing overshoes that kept sticking to the sidewalk! You wouldn't have been able to wear them in winter either. In the cold they got stiff and hard, and would break. You have already discovered this with your piece of waterproof cloth. But you know that your rubber boots don't behave this way. What makes the difference?

Place the band on a lighted light bulb for five minutes. Does the band get sticky like the piece of waterproof cloth did? Leave it overnight in the refrigerator freezer.

Hot and Cold Band

Things Needed:
Rubber band
Lamp with uncovered bulb
Freezer compartment of refrigerator

Does it become hard and brittle? You will find that the rubber band is quite different from your crude rubberized cloth.

A New England inventor, Charles Goodyear, spent five years trying to improve rubber clothing and solve the hot/cold problems. Finally, in 1839, he discovered a secret for curing rubber. His process is called *vulcanization*. Vulcanized rubber could be used in all kinds of weather. When the weather changed, the rubber didn't!

Vulcan was an ancient Roman god. He was the god of fire, and that should give you your first clue about vulcanization. Goodyear found that heat, at the correct temperature and for the right length of time, was one of the secrets of improving rubber. The other secret you've probably already guessed: it was sulphur.

A rubber band is still basically carbon and hydrogen. The addition of sulphur doesn't change its essential qualities . . . but it does make it perform a good deal better.

SHOWING WHAT YOU CAN'T SEE

You cannot see an atom. It is much too small. Someone once estimated that there are more than 1,000,000,000,000,000,000,000 atoms in a single drop of water. That's one sextillion atoms.

When two or more atoms join together, they form a molecule. These, too, are much too small to see. A rubber molecule contains five atoms of carbon and eight atoms of hydrogen. This molecule, made of thirteen atoms, is so tiny that it would require more than 25 million of them, placed end to end, to measure an inch. Of course, many thousands of such molecules, grouped together, would finally be large enough to see.

Look at a rubber band. You cannot possibly see the individual molecules that make it up. You can observe some things about them, however. You can see what color they appear when grouped together, and you can prove that they are stretchy.

The scientist, using special instruments, has studied the molecules in a rubber band and can tell you many other facts about them. He could make a giant model of just one of the molecules and show you something you will never really see. You can make this same kind of model.

The scientist knows that there are five carbon atoms and eight hydrogen atoms in the rubber molecule. He would write the formula C_5H_8. He might put a small n after the formula, like this: $(C_5H_8)n$. This n has a special meaning; we'll learn what it is a bit later. But just knowing what atoms are in the molecule, and how many of each, is not enough to make a model. You have to hitch them together in the correct way as well.

Make a Rubber Molecule Model

Things Needed:
Five black gumdrops
Eight white gumdrops
Fourteen toothpicks

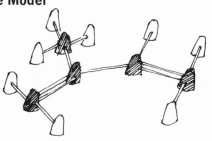

You can use any kind of small ball-shaped objects to represent the atoms, but gumdrops are easy to work with. Be sure to use two different colors: five of one color to stand for carbon atoms, and eight of another color to represent hydrogen atoms. Arrange the balls and toothpicks as in the illustration.

The toothpicks would not appear in a real rubber molecule. They represent *chemical bonds*. These are strong forces within the atoms. They attract other atoms, and cause them to stick together. The attraction of certain atoms for others, and the various ways they link together, are the basic principles of the science of chemistry. They can be used to explain why a substance appears and acts the way it does. Molecule models are one way a chemist studies these principles and perhaps makes new discoveries about chemical substances.

You will notice that you have used two toothpicks near both ends of your model. These represent special double bonds. This double strength isn't really necessary to hold the molecule together at these points; in fact, the additional bond can be used to attach something else to the molecule. If you picture your molecule as a long rope, these double bonds would be like little hooks hanging off the rope. If another atom or molecule is added in the right way, one of the double bonds may break and form a hook that catches it. This is the way a new compound is formed, either naturally or by the chemist.

Besides being fun to make, molecule models like this one can reveal many things about a substance: what atoms it is made of, how many of each atom it contains, how to write the formula for it, and how the attractions of the atoms act on each other.

If you would like to label your model, here are three different ways you might do it:

$(C_5H_8)n$

Or, you might choose to draw it . . .

```
              H
              |
  H    H—C—H    H         H
  |      |       |         |
  C======C———————C=========C
  |                        |
  H                        H
```

Or, you might use a combination of both . . .

```
            CH_3
             |
  CH_2=======C———————CH=======CH_2
```

Study each of these "different" methods and you can see how every one "says" exactly the same things!

Now what about that little n? This is an important symbol for understanding why the rubber molecule makes a piece of rubber the way it is. In the second and third methods of labeling your model the n was shown by drawing a double bond. Can you now guess what it means? It indicates, to the chemist, that the molecule has a further attraction for other similar molecules. If you wished to make another rubber molecule model, you could attach the two together by breaking one of the double bonds to provide you with a "hook". In a rubber band, thousands of such molecules are hitched together to make giant molecules. These giant molecules, made of thousands of similar smaller units, are called *polymers*. Thousands of these stringy polymers, side by side and woven together, make up the rubber band.

SYNTHETIC RUBBER

Rubber has become such an important material that now there are not enough rubber trees to supply the world's needs.

After the chemical make-up of rubber was discovered, many scientists tried to duplicate the rubber molecule in their laboratories using other chemicals. They knew that rubber was a *hydrocarbon* (chemicals made of hydrogen and carbon), as were coal and oil. They tried to rearrange the molecules of coal and oil to produce real rubber or a rubber-like chemical. Finally, in 1922, a gas called *butadiene* was produced from oil. This chemical, though a gas, has a long molecule that is something like rubber.

Make a Model Butadiene Molecule

Things Needed:
Four black gumdrops
Six white gumdrops
Eleven toothpicks

As with your rubber molecule, you can choose any of three labels for this molecule:

$(C_4H_6)n$

$$\begin{array}{cccccccc}
H & & H & & H & & H \\
| & & | & & | & & | \\
C & = & C & - & C & = & C \\
| & & & & & & | \\
H & & & & & & H
\end{array}$$

$$CH_2 = CH - CH = CH_2$$

By adding other chemicals to this gas, very rubber-like materials can be man-made in the laboratory. For example, the gas butadiene and the liquid *styrene* together produce a synthetic white latex that can be used like real latex to make paints, shoe soles, handbags, suitcases, automobile tires and hundreds of other useful articles. This rubber is called rubber-styrene, or GR-S (government rubber-styrene).

Other discoveries have resulted in a variety of new man-made rubbers. Scientists have even duplicated the real rubber molecule in their laboratories. Because of these discoveries, rubber trees now produce about half of the world's rubber . . . the other half comes out of test tubes!

3

Rubber Bands
in the Stretch

The one thing rubber bands do best is stretch. We take it for granted; after all, a rubber band wouldn't be of much use if it didn't stretch . . . but have you ever wondered how? Let's take a more careful look at the stretch in the rubber band. It follows certain science laws, and yet behaves in ways which are most peculiar.

Some scientists like to think of rubber as being made of long strings. These strings are twisted and bent. When you pull on the ends, you simply unbend and untwist the strands. When you release the ends, they return to their kinked and twisted shape. As long as the strands do not lose their kinks the band will be stretchy.

Light a match and hold it against the rubber band. As soon as the band starts to melt, blow the match out. Do not allow the band to catch fire or melt all the way through. While the band is still hot, try stretching it

Killing the Kinks

Things Needed:
Rubber band
A match

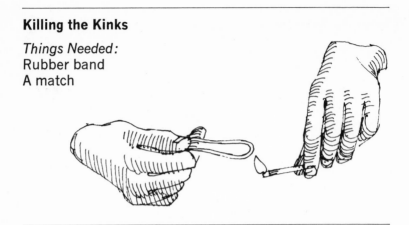

out. You will find the band is no longer elastic when it has been heated. The structure of the rubber has been changed, and the twists and bends of the rubber strands can no longer return to their original shapes.

Has the elastic quality been permanently removed at the place where the band was heated? Let a heated band cool down for an hour or so, then try to stretch it. Does it stretch after being cooled, or is the elastic quality really gone?

When you stretch a rubber band you must do a bit of work. The kinky strands resist being straightened out. You have to use some of your energy to do it. Your energy becomes heat energy in the band, and you can prove it.

Before stretching the band, touch it to your lips. Now stretch the band tightly between your hands, and quickly touch it again to your lips. The band will now feel quite a bit warmer! The energy you used to stretch

Stretch the Temperature

Things Needed:
Rubber band

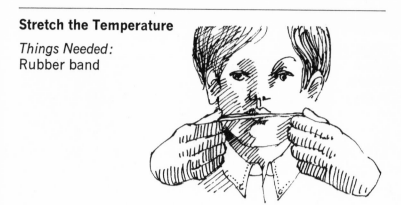

the band has changed to heat. Relax the band, and touch it to your lips once again. You will find it is now much cooler, almost cold. In the relaxed position the rubber band releases the heat energy. To make it warm again you must again stretch it, and again use a bit of your energy.

RUBBER BANDS ARE ELASTIC BANDS

You have probably called rubber bands "elastic bands" without thinking about the meaning of the phrase; but do the words "rubber" and "elastic" mean the same thing?

The word rubber tells you what the bands are made of, while the word *elastic* actually describes a particular quality about them. We can say that rubber is elastic, but we cannot say that all elastics are rubber. What, then, is an elastic?

An Elastic Quiz

Things Needed:
None . . . just think about
  each of the following:
Rubber band
Piece of wire
Strip of wood
Piece of glass
Glob of clay

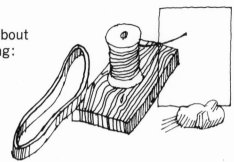

Only one item in the list is not an elastic; all the rest are. By comparing each with the rubber band, can you decide which is the non-elastic?

When you pull a rubber band, you apply a force that changes the shape of the band. As long as the force of your pulling continues, the band will keep its longer shape, but when you release your grip the force is eliminated and the band pops back to its original shape. Any material that can be distorted by a force, but resumes its original shape when the force is removed, is called an elastic. This is your first clue; but none of the materials on the list spring back like a rubber band, so you might still find it difficult to identify the one odd material.

Things can be elastic in several different ways. When you pull a rubber band you are experimenting with elastic *extension* (getting longer). If you pulled a wad of bubble gum between your fingers it would display extension, but it would not be elastic because the gum would not return to its original shape.

You can also change the shape of something by squeezing it. The squeeze is the force, and it is called *compression*. If you squeeze a rubber ball you will observe a perfect example of elastic compression. In fact, it is because of compression that a ball bounces when it is tossed on the floor. When the ball strikes the floor it is squeezed flat on the bottom, and bulges out the sides. Because it is elastic, it quickly rounds out again into its original shape. In doing this, it pushes off the floor and back up into the air. Can you imagine trying to bounce a ball made of chewing gum? It certainly would be distorted when it hit the floor, but, not being elastic, would not return to its original shape, so it could never bounce back up.

You can also twist an elastic material. You can twist a rubber band around and around until you have a tiny ball of rubber . . . let it go, and it pops back into shape. Twisting is called *torsion*.

And one last way you might distort an elastic would be by bending it. This is called *flexure*.

So, an elastic is something that can be pulled (extension), squeezed (compression), twisted (torsion) or bent (flexure), and it will resume its original shape when the force is removed. Which one on the list won't do that?

Surprisingly, wire will do it. So will wood and glass. But clay will not! Clay is the odd one. It remains in whatever shape you pull or squeeze, twist or bend it. Clay is a non-elastic.

THE ELASTIC LIMIT

It is difficult to think of things like glass or metal as being elastic like rubber. Glass breaks if we apply too much force . . . for instance, hitting a window with a baseball. A piece of wire stays bent if you fold it over. Some materials, like glass and metal, require a great deal of force to start them bending or twisting. Strangely enough, this resistance to being deformed also proves that they are elastic. Elastic things resist changing their shapes. When they have changed, and the force is released, they will return to their original shapes if the change is not too great. Otherwise, they will remain permanently bent, or they will break.

A Rubber Band and a Paper Clip

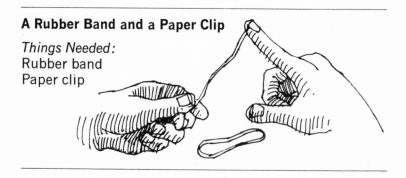

Things Needed:
Rubber band
Paper clip

Bend the paper clip out straight for this investigation. Both the band and the clip are similar in being elastics, but you would probably guess that the band seems much better at it. Try bending the clip, then the band. Which one requires the greatest force to cause it to bend? The force required to distort anything is called the *stress*. The clip is actually very elastic because it requires a great stress to deform it. Thinking of elastic things in this way, you might say that the clip is more elastic than the rubber band, because less force is needed to bend the band than the clip. But this is only part of the story.

Bend the clip a little bit and release it. It will spring back straight, if you have not bent it too far. Try again, bending it just a bit further. Keep bending until it does not spring back, but remains bent. When this happens, you have gone beyond the *elastic limit* of the metal in the clip.

Even if you fold the band over, and press it flat at the fold, it will spring back when you release it. The rubber band has a very high elastic limit, and the metal clip has a very low one. Therefore, thinking of elastic things in terms of how far they can be distorted and still return to their shapes, the rubber is much better than the metal.

From this investigation you have found that the elasticity of a material depends both on how much force is required to distort it, and how far it can be distorted before it reaches its elastic limit. An engineer, choosing a building material, would study both very carefully before beginning his construction.

A tall skyscraper must be elastic. The wind will blow against it and bend it back and forth. If the skyscraper were made of a non-elastic material, the wind would bend it and it would remain tilted to one side. If the building were constructed of a material like glass, which has a very low elastic limit, the first wind might snap it in two. The builder would not choose rubber either. Although a rubber building would always return to its original shape when the wind stopped blowing, only a small stress from a gentle breeze would be needed to cause the building to bend. The builder would definitely choose some material, like steel or wood, which requires a great stress to start it bending, and continues to resist as the wind blows stronger; yet, if the wind blows hard enough, the steel will be elastic enough to bend a bit and still return to its upright position later.

Because of the importance of the elasticity of materials to the engineer, great testing machines have been made to discover the elastic limits of all sorts of building materials. These machines pull, squeeze, twist, bend and finally break each of them to determine which one will do the best job in a bridge, skyscraper, house, automobile, or submarine.

THE LAW OF STRETCH

There are two different kinds of laws. One is a man-made law, such as a speed limit or a no-parking restriction. You can break these laws. If you do, you might have to pay a fine, go to court, or spend some time in jail, but you can break these laws! The other kind cannot be broken. These are called *natural laws*, or the laws of nature. They do not order things to behave in certain ways like man-made laws; rather, they explain how things do behave. When things always behave in the same way we say they are following laws, or rules, of nature.

Why, even a rubber band follows natural laws. No matter how big or small, fat or thin a rubber band may be, it will always stretch in the same way. The law it follows was discovered by a scientist named Robert Hooke and, in his honor, it is called Hooke's Law, or the law of stretch.

Discover the Law of Stretch

Things Needed:
Thin rubber band
Twelve-inch ruler
Two paper clips
Sticky tape
Two tablespoons, both the
    same size and weight

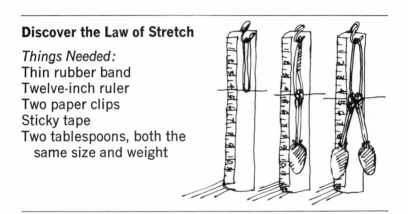

Clip one of the paper clips over the end of the ruler. Hook the rubber band over this clip. Clip the other paper clip over the end of the rubber band that is hanging down. Pull the band down along the ruler and note how long it is when it is not stretched. Be sure not to stretch it at all while making this measurement.

Hang one tablespoon on the paper clip at the free end of the rubber band, using the sticky tape to hold it. The weight of the spoon will cause the band to stretch. Note the new mark for the length of the band. Subtract your original, non-stretched, measurement from this one to learn how many inches (or what part of an inch) the weight of the spoon has caused the band to stretch.

Now fasten the second spoon to the first with the tape. Read the new measurement for the weight of both spoons and, again, subtract the original from it. Here is an example:

Unstretched band measures 4 inches
One spoon stretches it to $4\frac{1}{4}$ inches

$$\begin{array}{r} 4\frac{1}{4} \\ -4 \\ \hline \frac{1}{4} \end{array}$$ inch stretch with one spoon

Unstretched band measures 4 inches
Two spoons stretch it to $4\frac{1}{2}$ inches

$$\begin{array}{r} 4\frac{1}{2} \\ -4 \\ \hline \frac{1}{2} \end{array}$$ inch stretch with two spoons

From these figures you will discover that adding a second spoon stretched the band twice as far. Your measurements will probably be different from these, because you might use a smaller or larger band, but you will still discover that two spoons, of equal weights, will always stretch the band just twice as far as one will.

If you add another spoon, the three spoons will stretch the band three times as far as the stretch of one. Four spoons, four times as far, and so forth.

This then is Hooke's Law, the law of stretch. Scientifically, Hooke's Law says that strain is directly proportional to stress. Stress, you will remember, is the force pulling on the band. In this investigation, the stress is the weight of the spoons. Strain is the amount that the band is deformed, or stretched. Proportional simply means that if you double the stress, you will also double the strain. Twice the weight makes twice the stretch.

Remember, this is not true just for rubber bands. This is a scientific law that holds true for all elastic materials. If the wind blows twice as hard at a skyscraper, the building will bend twice as far. To stretch a metal spring twice as far, you will have to pull it just twice as hard.

There is a way to break the law. Perhaps you've already guessed it. If you go beyond the elastic limit, the stretch is gone, and the law won't work. But think about this for a moment. Is this really breaking the law?

If you truly understand the law of stretch, perhaps you might enjoy ending with an easy puzzle to solve. If a one pound weight stretches a rubber band five inches, and a two pound weight stretches it ten inches, how far will it stretch if we hang a ten pound weight on it? How about a three and one-half pound weight?

WHEN THE BAND'S HOT

Have you ever tried to open a jar, only to discover that the cover was on too tight and wouldn't turn? Perhaps, after you tried to be a strong man and failed, your mother did it easily by holding the cover under hot water for a moment. Possibly your mother didn't realize it, but she was applying a science principle.

Most materials, like the metal in a jar cover, *expand* and get bigger when they are heated. The bearings in an automobile must have oil. If they don't they will get hot, expand, and lock or "freeze" in place. Bridges and railroad tracks have little spaces between the joints which allow the metal to expand during hot weather. Even gases expand when they are heated. A balloon filled with air gets bigger if it is placed in a pan of hot water. Liquids expand also. That is why the liquid in a thermometer moves up the glass tube as the temperature rises.

It is almost a rule that things expand when they are heated; it is almost a rule, but there are a few odd exceptions. A piece of rubber is one. If you heat a piece of rubber it will *contract* and get smaller!

A Moving Knot

Things Needed:
Rubber band
Piece of wood, about one foot long
Two thumbtacks

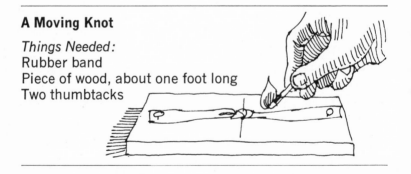

Cut the band to make a long strip of rubber. Tie a knot in the center. Push one tack into one end of the board and tie an end of the band to it. Tie the other end of the band to the other thumbtack. Stretch the band down the board until it is quite tight, then push the thumbtack in place to hold it. With a pencil, mark the board right beside the knot.

Now, bring a lighted match close to the band between the knot and one end of the board. Do not touch or burn the band with the match. Watch the knot. You will discover that the knot moves toward the match as the band is heated. If you move the match to the opposite end, the knot will move back toward the match.

The knot moves toward the side that is heated because heated rubber contracts. The heat causes that side of the band to become shorter.

Why does rubber behave in this odd way? One idea is that it becomes shorter by contraction, but, at the same time, it becomes fatter by expansion. If that sounds confusing, you might think of all the rubber molecules that make up the band as being links in long chains. If you spread a real chain across a table and started shaking one end, the other end would be drawn toward you as the links began to overlap. Applying heat to a rubber band causes the rubber molecule chains to vibrate in the same way. In taking up more space to each side, the ends of the molecule chains are pulled closer together. This makes the band get shorter, and fatter, both at the same time.

Here is another device that shows the contraction of a rubber band. The rubber band only contracts a tiny bit, but by adding a paper clip you are able to magnify the motion.

Rubber Band Heat-O-Meter

Things Needed:
Rubber band
Drinking glass
Paper clip
Matches

Loop the band around the top of the drinking glass. Bend the inside end of the paper clip so that it is pointing straight down. Slip the end of the clip under the band, so that the band presses it against the glass. The rest of the clip is now up above the glass and will become the pointing needle for your heat-o-meter. Be sure that the long side of the clip is pointing out away from the glass.

Bring a lighted match close to the band on one side of the paper clip. You will find that the clip will swing around and point toward the lighted match. Your heat-o-meter is an instrument that can detect, and point out, heat. It will always point in the direction the heat is coming from.

You can also make your meter point away from the heat, simply by turning the clip so that it is over the glass rather than pointing out from it.

If you are an "inventor," perhaps you might like to try making a thermometer from a rubber band. The band will become shorter as the temperature rises, and longer as the temperature drops. Remember that you cannot use your heat-o-meter for this, because the band on both sides of the clip will always be the same temperature. If you can invent a way of arranging the needle and the band so that the needle would move with changes in temperature, you could write down the correct temperatures beside the needle by comparing it with a real thermometer. How to arrange the band and the clip to do this makes an interesting problem to leave with you.

4

A Musical (Rubber) Band

Suppose someone asked you to make a musical sound. What would you need to make it?

You wouldn't have to know a song!

You wouldn't need any practice!

You wouldn't need an expensive instrument!

The first thing you would need would be a definition. Just what is a musical sound?

A musical sound is not music! Music is a great many musical sounds arranged in a pleasing way. Only a skilled musician can make music, but anyone can make a musical sound. You do not have to have any instruments, because practically anything can make a musical sound. Often things can make only one note. One note cannot make music, but one note is still a musical sound.

All sounds in our world might be divided into two groups. Either they are musical sounds, or they are noise. If you tap the side of a drinking glass it produces a musical, bell-like, sound. If you accidentally dropped the glass, it would make a lot of noise as it broke on the floor. What is the difference?

Perhaps, before asking this question, we should remind ourselves of what makes a sound. Sound is produced by something vibrating. Drumheads, guitar strings, and the air inside a trumpet all vibrate and make sounds. Vocal cords in your throat vibrate when you talk or sing. The sides of a glass vibrate when you tap it, and the pieces vibrate all over the floor if you drop it. For every sound, musical or not, there must be a vibration.

SOUND—NOISE AND MUSIC

There are many ways to cause a rubber band to vibrate and create a sound. Most, you will find, are quite musical.

Band Music

Things Needed:
Rubber band

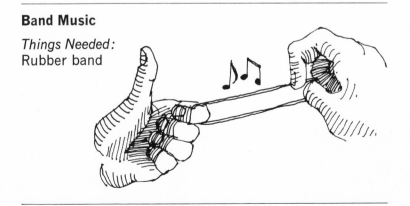

Stretch a rubber band between your hands and pluck it with your thumb. Can you hear a musical note? There are some other ways to make the band "sing," too. With the band stretched tight, pull the middle of it along the edge of a desk or table. Pull out a desk drawer and stretch the band over it; then gently rub a pencil back and forth, like a violin bow, over the middle of the band.

Carefully watch the rubber band vibrating as you try each of these methods. Can you notice that it vibrates evenly? When an object vibrates evenly, with the same number of vibrations each second, it has a musical sound. Now can you guess what a noise is?

A Noisy Band

Things Needed:
Rubber band

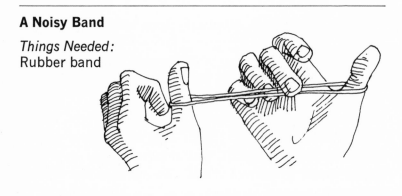

Hold the band with one hand so that it hangs loosely. Pull it back with your other hand and let it snap. Is this a musical sound? Now, loop the band over your palm and pluck it anywhere you like. Each time you pluck, the band slaps back against your hand. But it does not sound musical.

Neither of these methods allows the band to vibrate in an even way. There is a sharp vibration of the air, but the vibrations do not continue; therefore they are not even. Musical sounds are steady, even vibrations. Noise may be either a single sharp vibration, or many uneven ones.

BIG SOUNDS—LITTLE SOUNDS

If you wished to make musical sounds for a large audience, you probably would not use a rubber band stretched between your hands. You could still use a rubber band, if you added just one other part to your instrument.

The rubber band, by itself, does not make a loud enough sound. A scientist refers to the loudness of sound as *volume*. To make a sound, the band must vibrate the air around it. The vibrating air then passes the sound to your ear in much the same way as a wave travels in the water. The rubber band is narrow, so the wave it produces is also small. This small wave cannot strike your eardrum with very much energy. You hear it as a sound with low volume. To increase the volume you must create a stronger wave. A common way to do this is to add a *sounding board*.

Guitar strings, piano wires, and violin strings are not large enough to create a sound wave with enough volume to fill a concert hall; but, with the assistance of a sounding board, they do it easily. You can too, with your rubber band.

Add a Sounding Board

Things Needed:
Rubber band
Small cardboard box

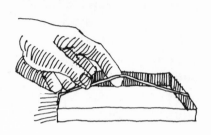

Loop the band around the box. Pluck the band in the center on the open side of the box, and you will discover the sound is much louder.

You have increased the volume by causing more air to vibrate. The band passes its vibrations along to the box. Parts of the box are also set into vibration. Naturally, the air surrounding the box also vibrates. Because the box is much larger than the band, more air is now vibrating and passing the sound waves to your ear. These bigger waves make the sound louder than before.

The Sounding Board Vibrates

Things Needed:
Rubber band
Small cardboard box
Salt

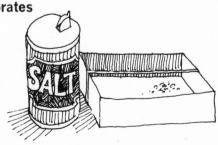

Pour just a tiny bit of salt into the bottom of the box. The band should be looped around as in the previous investigation. Pluck the band and observe the salt grains carefully. You will find that the salt dances about the bottom of the box each time you pluck. The salt is responding, like the invisible air molecules, to the vibrations of the cardboard sounding board. Tip the box on its side, and turn it in different directions as you pluck the band. Does the salt jump in every spot, or are there some places where the box does not seem to be vibrating?

If you are a careful observer you will find several places which do not vibrate. These are called *nodes*. Sounding boards differ a great deal in their abilities to pick up the tiny vibrations from a string or rubber band. We might say that the sounding board has a "personality." It may be a good sounding board with a pleasing personality, or it may have a bad one. This personality is due, in part, to where the nodes form.

Pick the Best Personality

Things Needed:
Several different sounding boards
   (paper cup, plastic cup,
   tin can, boxes of different kinds
   of cardboard, etc.)
Rubber bands of the same kind,
   one for each sounding board

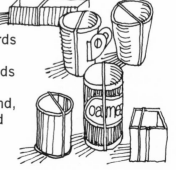

Loop a band over each sounding board. Pluck the bands and listen to the sounds. You will find that each board sounds different from the others.

You can purchase a fine wooden violin and pay several thousand dollars for it. You can also buy one for less than one hundred dollars. You might also go to a toy store and buy a plastic violin that looks just like the expensive ones, for just a few dollars.

Why would anyone want to pay a thousand dollars for a violin? Perhaps you realize now that there is much more to a musical instrument than just its appearance. The material used to make it is very important. Properly resonant material, and care in the making, will result in a better sounding board which can pick up even the slightest vibrations and make them loud. In a fine violin, the type of wood it is made from, the thickness of the wood in different parts of the instrument, and even the kind of glue used to hold it together, are carefully chosen to produce the most pleasing sounds.

You will be using your one-band musical sound maker for several more investigations, so now is a good time to select the very best sounding board for these future investigations. You may not achieve the sound quality of a fine violin, but you can be certain that your friends will appreciate your effort to choose with care.

HIGH SOUNDS—LOW SOUNDS

A musical instrument requires just three things. Two you have already investigated. First it requires something that vibrates evenly . . . the rubber band. Second, it requires something to make the vibrations stronger . . . a sounding board. Finally, it must have a way of making different notes. Most instruments are able to make high sounds and low sounds as they are needed. The note is called *pitch*, *tone*, or, scientifically, *frequency*. Thus far, your rubber band instrument has provided you with only one note, but there are three different ways to make it produce others.

How Hard You Pull

Things Needed:
Rubber band
Small cardboard box

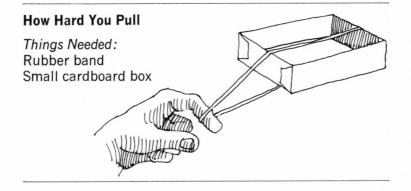

Loop the band around the sounding board box. Hold the box in one hand and the rubber band in the other. Pull the band out away from the box and pluck it with the thumb of the hand holding the band. You will hear a note. To change the note, move your hand closer to the box as you pluck. Then move it further away.

The tighter you pull the band, the higher the frequency. The less you pull, the lower the frequency.

A guitar player must tune his guitar by stretching the strings just the right amount. He does this by wrapping the strings around pegs in the handle. He must stretch the strings to a *tension* that will produce just the right note.

Tension, or tightness, is the first method of making notes high and low.

How Long the String

Things Needed:
Rubber band
Small cardboard box

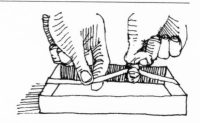

For this investigation you must not change the tension on the band. Loop the band over the box and place the box flat on the table, open side up. Pluck the band, which now serves as a string, and listen to the note. Now grasp the center of the band tightly between your thumb and finger, and pluck the band on one side. Is the note higher or lower when only half the band vibrates?

Hold the band in other places and, while gripping it tightly, pluck again. You will notice that every time you change the length of the band you also change the frequency of the sound it makes. Changing the length of the band is the second way of making notes high and low.

If you have tried both of the previous investigations you might find yourself a bit confused. In the last, you found that as you made the band shorter the note went higher. But, in the first investigation, when you stretched the band longer the note went higher. Do not be confused by this. Remember, when you stretched the band longer it could not make a low sound because it was pulled tighter. If two bands were both pulled to the same tension but one was longer than the other, the longer one would always make the lower note. In real musical instruments, tension and length work together.

If you were to examine the strings on a guitar or violin you would find another factor that produces different notes. Some of the strings would be very thin, some fat, and some in between. The thickness of the string joins with tension and length to make different notes.

Fat and Thin Strings

Things Needed:
Two rubber bands
   (one "fat," one "thin")
Small cardboard box

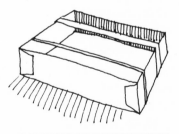

Loop the bands around the box so that they are side by side, and pluck each of them. You will make two different notes with the two bands, which now serve as strings, while both are the same length and at about the same tension!

Which is harder to start moving, a roller skate or an automobile? The heavier an object is, the harder it is to start moving. The fatter band is hard to start because it is heavier. Imagine what is happening when a band vibrates. It starts, moves up ... stops ... starts and moves down ... stops ... starts and moves up ... and so on. Don't you suppose a thin band, being lighter, would have an easier time starting and stopping than a heavy fat one? Therefore, another rule is: the thicker the band (string), the lower the note. A lower note is made by fewer vibrations (starts and stops) per second.

Because size, length, and tension all work together to determine a string's note, you might enjoy playing with different combinations to see what different notes you can make. To get started, try looping a small and a large band around the box. Pull the fat band and make it tighter. By plucking, listening, and pulling, can you make the fat band produce a note as high as the thin one?

Now try making the two bands produce the same note by holding the fat one at different places as you did in the How Long the String investigation.

Arrange the small band around the box so that it is very loose over the opening in the box. With less tension it will make a lower note. Pull the fat band tighter around the box. This will cause the fat band to make a higher note. Now, by carefully arranging the two bands, try to make both produce the same note.

LET'S MAKE MUSIC

Do you know what music is? Music is putting together different musical sounds in a way that is pleasing to our ears.

Here's an assortment of high and low notes that are ear-pleasing and arranged in an order that seems to fit together:

Mary Had a Little Lamb

Let's learn how to play it, and use a bit of science and mathematics at the same time. First you will need an instrument. It must have a string, sounding board, and some notes.

A Rubber Band-jo

Things Needed:
Thin rubber band
Two thumbtacks
Piece of wood twenty inches long
Small cardboard box,
    about three inches wide

Push a thumbtack into each end of the board. Cut the band to make a long string and tie one end to one of the thumbtacks. Pull the band down along the board and tie the other end to the opposite tack. Push both tacks in hard to hold the band tightly. Lift the band at one end and slide the box under to act as a sounding board. If you now pluck the band you will hear a musical note. But your instrument must still be tuned.

The note you make depends on the length, size and tension of the band. You cannot easily change the size because you have used a thin band and fastened it in place. You can, however, change the length simply by sliding the box under the band closer to the end. Slide the box along until it is exactly 14 inches away from one end of the band. You will understand why 14 inches is important a bit later.

You can also change the tension of the band, by pulling out a tack a bit and wrapping some of the band around it. This is the method we will use to tune the Band-jo.

We would like to tune the string to vibrate exactly 256 times a second. This tone is called *Middle C*. Middle C is one of the many frequencies that musicians have found very pleasing to our ears. The easiest way to tune your instrument to this frequency is to play Middle C on a piano while adjusting the tension on the band. When both produce the same note your Band-jo is in tune. (If you are not familiar with a piano, but can use one in school or at a friend's house, Middle C is the 24th white key from the left of the keyboard.)

If you cannot tune your Band-jo to a piano, simply tune it to a note that is pleasing to your ear. This may disturb a few music lovers when you finally play "Mary Had a Little Lamb," but you will still find it sounds good to you.

Once your Band-jo is tuned to vibrate 256 times a second, at Middle C, you will still not be able to play a song. To play "Mary Had a Little Lamb" you will require the note you have, plus three others: D, E, and G. Each of these letters represents a note made by a different number of vibrations per second. Altogether, they are part of a musical *scale*. This scale, and the number of vibrations for each note, would be:

Middle							High
C	D	E	F	G	A	B	C
256	288	324	342	384	432	486	512

You probably also know these notes by their syllable names. You would sing them:

Middle							High
C	D	E	F	G	A	B	C
Do	Re	Mi	Fa	Sol	La	Ti	Do

And, in written music, they would appear:

To play "Mary Had a Little Lamb," you must make the band vibrate at four different speeds: 256 times a second for C, 288 times a second for D, 324 times a second for E, and 384 vibrations a second for G. How can you do it?

You cannot change the tightness or size quickly as you are playing. This leaves just one method . . . change the length of the band!

In assembling your Band-jo you arranged the band to be exactly 14 inches long. Then you tuned it to vibrate 256 times each second. If you place a pencil on the exact center of the string (seven inches) and press down hard you "cut the band in half." When you pluck it between the box and the pencil it will vibrate faster . . . in fact, just twice as fast because it is just half as long. The band now vibrates 512 times a second which, you will notice, is called High C.

If you continue plucking while you slide the pencil down the band you will hear the note drop lower. Between the center of the band and the end are all the notes you need. How do you find them?

Putting Notes on Your Band-jo

Things Needed:
Rubber band-jo
Twelve-inch ruler
Pencil

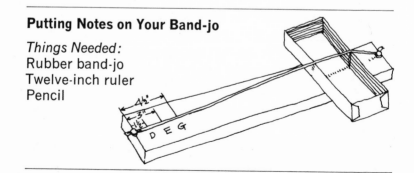

Measure in $1\frac{1}{2}$ inches from the end of the board opposite the cardboard box. Make a mark here, and label it D. Measure 3 inches from the end of the board and mark this E. Measure in $4\frac{1}{2}$ inches from the end and mark this G. You now have all the notes you require to play "Mary Had a Little Lamb."

Music from Musical Sounds

Things Needed:
Rubber band-jo with notes marked
Pencil
Song sheet

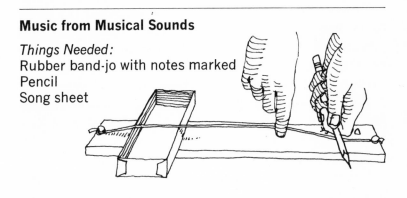

You already know how to play your Band-jo. Simply pluck the band; to change notes press the pencil down on a mark to change the band's length, and pluck the band. Remember, the one note you haven't marked is C, because that is the full length of the band.

To press correct notes at the correct times so that they fit together and make pleasing music, you must have a song sheet. The sheet can be the written music version with the different notes drawn on lines; or you might wish to use this version, which you can place close to your instrument:

Mary Had a Little Lamb

E D C D E E E   D D D   E G G
E D C D E E E E D D E D C

Once you have "mastered" your Band-jo, and
understand how the notes change as the band length
changes, you might attempt two more difficult tunes.
Besides requiring you to be a better musician, these
songs may require you to do a little musical manipulation before they sound right.

The songs are familiar to you:

Twinkle, Twinkle, Little Star

London Bridge Is Falling Down

If you try to play these tunes on your Band-jo you will discover that they include two notes you have not marked, F and A.

For F make a mark $3\frac{1}{2}$ inches in from the end of the board and for A make a mark $5\frac{3}{4}$ inches in. If, when trying these tunes, you strike a "sour" note which seems out of tune you must do some musical manipulation to correct it. Slide your pencil back and forth until you strike the note that does sound right. Sometimes your ear is the best for telling exactly where a mark should be. Mathematics has helped us determine where the notes should be but our measurements are not exact, and you must use your ear to decide where they should be.

Although the last two notes missing from the scale are not required for any of these tunes, you might wish to add B (a mark $6\frac{3}{8}$ inches from the end of the board) and High C (in the exact center, 7 inches in) to make it complete. Perhaps you can find a simple tune in a song book and try to play it on your Band-jo. You will discover there is a great difference between making musical sounds and making the sounds of music. You have experimented with only the barest essentials for music making. Perhaps a musical friend can show you even more you can do with your Rubber Band-jo.

FOR THE MUSICAL MATH MINDED

After playing the tunes, you might wonder just how we know where to draw the marks to cause the band to vibrate at the proper rate to produce the different notes.

It was not done "by ear"; it was done with mathematics.

Although music depends a good deal on our ear and what sounds good, it also could be studied by a deaf person . . . if he were clever with mathematics!

Here is the formula:

(note we want) × (length we want) =
(note we have) × (length we have)

We used a rubber band that was exactly 14 inches long. This is the "length we have." We tuned the band to Middle C, which is 256 vibrations a second. This 256 is the "note we have." When this information is added, the formula looks like this:

(note we want) × (length we want) = 256 × 14

Next we must select the "note we want" and include its vibrations per second in the formula:

D = 288 vibrations per second
E = 324 vibrations per second
F = 342 vibrations per second
G = 384 vibrations per second
A = 432 vibrations per second
B = 486 vibrations per second

Let's find out how long a string must be to produce the note E, which vibrates 324 times per second. Our formula for E would then look like this:

324 × (length we want) = 256 × 14 (which is 3584)

We divide the number on the right (3584) by the number on the left:

$$\text{length we want} = 324\overline{)3584}. = 11.06$$

So

length we want = 11.06 inches

Rounding this off to 11 inches means that the pencil must "cut off" 3 inches from the 14 inch band to leave the 11 inches. You will notice that you made your mark for E at 3 inches from the end of the board.

The mark for any other note would be found using this same formula. If you wished to make a bigger Band-jo, using a longer band, you could find the new marks by substituting the new length for the "length we have" in this same formula.

If you are math-minded you might enjoy working out the lengths for all of the notes on your 14-inch Band-jo. You will find some a bit different than the ones listed. Those listed were "rounded off" to make measuring easier. Perhaps you can calculate and measure them more exactly, and obtain more perfect notes.

5

Rubber Bands and You

Rubber bands are useful for many things. We've so far been considering the rubber band itself, its chemical makeup and its music. This chapter will remind you that rubber bands, like so many small household things, can be very useful to the amateur scientist as laboratory tools to help him learn more about the world. We can even use them to discover some odd facts about the most important subject in the world—you!

RUBBER BAND MUSCLES

A rubber band behaves a great deal like your muscles. Although your muscles are alive and the band isn't, they both do the same job of stretching and pulling. A rubber band cannot push anything; it can only pull. That's also true of a muscle.

Rubber Band Muscle Model

Things Needed:
Two three-inch-long rubber bands
A thumbtack or paper fastener
Piece of heavy cardboard,
   4″ × 6″ or larger

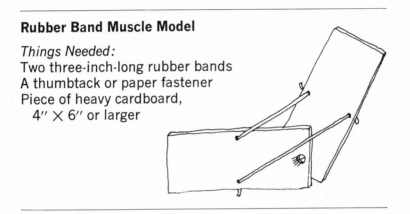

Cut the cardboard into two pieces, each six inches long and two inches wide, with rounded corners. Punch two holes in each piece, close to the edges and three inches from the end. Arrange the pieces as shown in the illustration, using the thumbtack or paper fastener to make the "joint." Cut the rubber bands to make long strips of rubber, and thread them through the holes; each band should go from a hole in one cardboard piece to the corresponding hole in the other piece. Tie knots in the ends of the bands to keep them from slipping through the holes. The cardboard pieces will represent bones, and the bands are the muscles.

If you have arranged the pieces exactly as shown, you will find you can make the rubber bands pull the "bones" in either direction just by giving them a slight push. You have to give a push to start it going; in a real muscle, the "push" is supplied by an order from your brain.

Every moving bone in your body has two or more muscles attached to it: one to pull it in one direction, and an opposing one to pull it back. Muscles, like rubber bands, can only pull; therefore, they must always work in pairs.

Here is an interesting question. Do you have muscles in your fingers to make them move? The answer might surprise you: you don't. Yet your fingers do move, and muscles do supply the power.

Muscle Power for a Finger Model

Things Needed:
Muscle model
Some heavy string

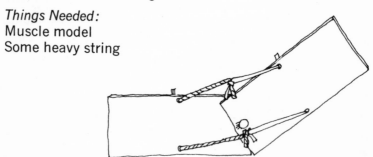

A Muscle Power for a Finger model will look just like the Rubber Band Muscle model, except that a piece of string will replace half of each band. Cut the bands in half and tie a piece of string about three inches long between the end of each band and one of the holes in the cardboard. The string cannot pull, but the band attached to it can. The two work together, with the band doing the pulling and the string carrying the pull to the "finger."

If you place your left hand fingers on the muscles in the lower part of your right arm, and wiggle your right fingers, you can probably feel the movement of the muscles. These muscles, in your arm, are attached to string-like *tendons* which carry the pull to all parts of your fingers. Because of this arrangement you have fingers that are both slender and powerful. If you did not have tendons, you'd have to have muscles in your fingers, and they'd be either so tiny and weak as to be practically useless for grasping or squeezing, or so big that your fingers would be "muscle-bound."

Of course, your arms, legs, and fingers don't whip back and forth like your rubber band models. Your muscles are different lengths and strengths, and provide different amounts of pull. Your joints allow your bones to move only in certain directions, and some only a small distance in any one direction. Your body is actually much more complicated than any model you could make; in a way, that only makes it more surprising that your muscles and rubber bands behave in such similar ways.

BRAIN POWER AND BRAWN POWER

Human hands are amazingly versatile tools. Think of all the jobs your hands do for you. They hold, grasp, feel, lift, turn, twist, shake, wiggle, and wave, to name just a few. There are so many things they can do very well that it might surprise you to find a few things they are not good at.

A Band on Your Hand

Things Needed:
Small rubber band

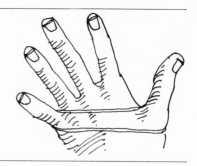

Loop the band around your little finger. Pull it over the back of your hand and loop the other end over your thumb. Pull the band down below your knuckles. Now, without using your other hand, and without rubbing the band against anything, try to work the band off your hand!

This can easily become the most frustrating trick you have tried. It is practically impossible to remove the band with the hand it is looped around. Why? Because to do it easily you would have to bend your fingers backwards. And they just don't bend that way.

A Band on Your Wrist

Things Needed:
Small rubber band

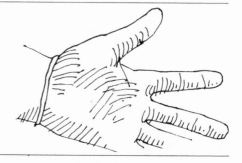

Loop the band around your wrist just below the base of your thumb. Using this same hand, try to remove the band. If you can do it you probably have very long fingers with very flexible joints. Most people cannot even touch their wrists with their fingers.

This might be called an experiment in *manual dexterity*. "Manual" is from the Latin word "manus," meaning "a hand," and "dexterity" means "a skill using one's body." Your manual dexterity, therefore, is how skillful you are with your hands.

If you try these investigations on your friends, you will discover some will be able to remove the bands while others will swear that it is impossible. Manual dexterity varies with different people.

Sometimes manual dexterity can be aided by using your brain. We might call this *mental dexterity*. Your brain cannot make your fingers bend backwards, but it does control them. Sometimes if you sit and think about a difficult task you may discover a simple solution to a problem your body is not able to overcome with sheer brawn. Perhaps, in the first investigation, you could work the band off by concentrating on rubbing it where it loops over your thumb, rather than by wiggling your whole hand. Could shaking it help? If your fingers are not nimble enough to remove the band, be sure to think about another solution before quitting.

HEART AT WORK

You cannot see your heart, but you can feel its pumping action. By placing your hand over your heart, you can feel your heart directly. As the heart forces blood through the large arteries, these tubes swell and shrink: if you press against one that is located close to the surface of your skin you may feel it throb. This throb is called a *pulse*. There are several places you might try:

Press your fingers in front of your ears, level with your eyes. Can you feel a pulse?

Try pressing in against the sides of your neck.

You should also feel it just above your collarbones on the front side of your shoulders.

Try pressing different places on your foot. You should find a good pulse there.

A doctor always uses his fingers rather than his thumb when taking a patient's pulse. There is a large artery in the thumb, and he might feel his own pulse instead of the patient's. Push your thumb down on a table and perhaps you can feel your own pulse there.

Probably you already know that the most common place to check a pulse is at the artery which is close to the skin at the wrist. By pressing down on the front side of your wrist you should be able to locate it. If you cannot find it easily it may be a bit deeper than most, but if you feel a strong beat, here is an investigation you might try to prove you are "heart at work."

Heart Beat-O-Meter

Things Needed:
Small rubber band
Wooden pencil

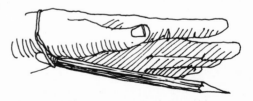

Locate the spot on your wrist where the pulse beat is strongest. Loop the band around your wrist. Place the eraser of the pencil directly over the pulse and slip the band over it so that the eraser is pressed hard into the pulse. You may have to double the band to assure that it presses quite firmly against your wrist.

Rest your elbow on the table and tip your hand forward so that the pencil extends outward as in the illustration. Hold your arm and hand very still. If the pencil and the band are properly arranged you will notice that the pencil is waving up and down in perfect rhythm with your heartbeat. If the pencil does not move, adjust the band and the pencil a bit. This is a rather difficult investigation; you may have to try several times before it works well, but once you find the right spot, it will be easy to do it again any time you wish. By using this investigation, you can find out a number of things about yourself and your friends.

What is your pulse rate? Is it 72 times a minute? Count the times the pencil jumps and see. You don't have to hold still for a full minute to do this. Just count the beats for 15 seconds (a quarter of a minute) and multiply the number by 4 to learn what it would be for a full minute. Probably your heartbeat will be faster than 72. As you grow older your heart will beat more slowly. Babies' hearts beat more than 100 times a minute; those of children may be anywhere between 72 and 92.

Here are some other facts you might check on:

- Women generally have a faster heart rate (between 70 and 80) than men (between 65 and 70).

- Your heart beats faster when you are standing than when you are lying down.

- Your heart beats faster after eating.

- Your heart beats faster after exercising.   (Run around the room a few times.)

- Your heart beats faster when you have a fever.

- And, the next time you get a good scare, if you check your heart rate I'm sure you will find it beating faster.

QUICKER THAN THE EYE

Have you ever watched a magician very closely? Even when you do, he can usually fool you with his sleight of hand. People say that a magician is able to fool us because his hand moves "quicker than the eye."

How quickly can you move your hand? Can you move it at a speed of 60 miles per hour? To do that, your hand will have to move a mile a minute. That really sounds impossible, and it is. But even if you could move your hand that fast, would you be unable to see it? Have you ever watched an automobile zoom past you at 60 miles an hour? Of course you have, and the car didn't disappear. You have probably seen things moving even faster than that. Jet airplanes fly at about 700 miles per hour, and you can still see them.

It is true, however, that our eyes do have difficulty observing things that are moving very quickly. Although you cannot move your hand fast enough to cause it to vanish, it can still become a blur that is confusing to our eyes. If you stretch a rubber band and let it go, you see it stretched and then loose, but you do not really see it moving when it snaps. This fact is the basis of an amusing science-magic trick.

Abracadabra Band

Things Needed:
Small rubber band

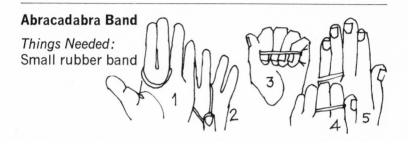

Loop the band around the bottom of the first two fingers on your right hand. Hold the band, on the palm side of your hand, and pull it forward. Fold all four fingers down inside the loop you've made and let the band go. It should rest across your fingernails. Now turn your hand over, holding it closed in a fist. You will notice that the band looks as though it is only looped around the first and second fingers.

Straighten your fingers and say abracadabra and the band will appear to jump from your first two fingers to the last two.

Practice this until you can do it perfectly, then show it to a friend.

You can also make the band jump back using the same method. Start with the band on your last two fingers instead of the first two.

Does the band really move quicker than your eye? You may find, if you watch very closely, that you can see a blur as the band snaps. It doesn't really move at a speed impossible to follow. It fools us because it takes us by surprise. It will fool your friends because they do not know what is going to happen.

Your eye is much too fine a "camera" to be fooled by rapid motion. Your brain, however, is easily confused by a magician, because everything he does is a surprise. He may also use misleading motions or words to make you look somewhere else at the crucial moment. Surprise, misdirection, and skill help the magician; every magician, like every scientist, knows that his hand cannot move too fast for an eye to see. The best magicians always fool our brains, not our eyes.

RIGHT TO YOUR EAR

Imagine that sound waves are like waves in water. If you drop a stone into a quiet pond, tiny waves travel outward from the center of disturbance. If you think of the dropped stone as a vibrating rubber band, and the water as the air around it, it is easy to picture sound waves spreading outward through the air from a vibrating band. Of course, waves travel on the flat surface of the water, and there is air all around the rubber band, so you'll have to do a little more imagining to picture the sound waves traveling out in all directions, to the sides, up, and down all at the same time; but thinking of the pond should help you to understand what's happening in the next few investigations.

If you were to throw a stone into the middle of a pond, and place your hand in the water near the edge, the wave from the stone would eventually strike your hand. Of course, that would only be a tiny bit of the entire wave the stone makes; the rest would be moving toward the other shores of the pond.

When a sound wave moves outward from a vibrating object, only a tiny bit of the wave enters your ear. The rest continues to spread out just like the water wave, except it is spreading in all directions.

Actually this is a very good thing! When your teacher talks to your class you can hear very well, and so can all of your classmates. Her voice travels outward in every direction so everyone is able to catch a bit and hear what is being said. If sound traveled in only one direction, and she spoke to you, nobody else would hear, and you would probably be deafened by the roar of her voice! An easy way to appreciate this fact is to

A Band in Your Ear

Things Needed:
Rubber band

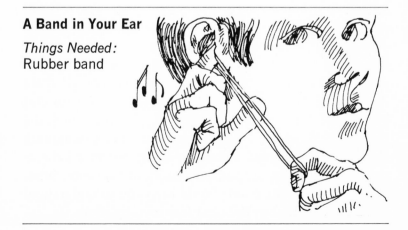

direct a vibration straight into your ear. If you use a tiny sound, you might be surprised by how loud it sounds. To make A Band in Your Ear do the following.

Loop the band over a finger on each hand and pluck it gently. Practice plucking until the sound it makes is almost too soft to hear. Now put one end of the looped band into your ear, as shown. Pluck it again, as gently as before. This time it should sound very loud. You will find that you can even hear the sound of your fingers rubbing on the band. If you pluck it very hard, it will probably be too uncomfortable to listen to; yet if you remove the band from your ear and pluck it just as hard, it will sound quite soft.

In this investigation you concentrated the sound by placing the source of vibration inside your ear. This made almost all the air vibration take place right beside your hearing organs; very little of it escaped beyond the shell of your ear to spread out in all directions. Distance was important—the closer you are to a noise the louder it sounds—but the fact that the sound waves were trapped in a small space, where they couldn't spread and fade but could only bounce back on each other, was even more significant.

Vibrations travel much better through hard materials than through the air. You can hear a train coming by placing your ear against the track, long before you hear it when you are standing up. Indians used to place their ears on the ground to hear approaching horses for this same reason. Because sound travels best through solid materials, you can hear a loud sound from a rubber band by using your very solid skull bones!

Using Your Head

Things Needed:
Rubber band
Two pieces of cotton

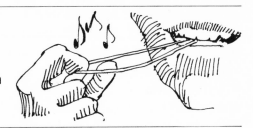

Put cotton in each ear. Then grip one end of the band in your teeth. Pull the other end out with your hand. Pluck the band and you can hear the sound clearly.

We often think of our ears as the flaps sticking out of the sides of our heads, but these are really rather insignificant as far as hearing is concerned. The flap is a funnel that collects the sound. The actual "hearing" part of the ear is inside. On each side of the head there is a small hole in the skull, with an *eardrum* stretched across it. The eardrum vibrates in time with the entering sound waves and passes the vibrations to three tiny bones, the smallest bones in your body, called the *hammer, anvil,* and *stirrup.* These work together to make the vibrations stronger, and pass them to the *cochlea.* This organ contains the nerves that send signals to the brain. Except for the flap, every part of your ear is inside the skull bone.

In this investigation you simply by-passed the funnel. The vibrations of the band were passed to your skull and then passed directly to the important parts of your ear. You heard the vibrations as quite loud sounds because sound travels even better through your solid skull than through the air.

This method of transmitting sounds to your ears is called *bone conduction*. Bone conduction is sometimes used by people who are hard of hearing. These people wear a tiny hearing aid behind their ears. The device picks up sound waves from the air through a tiny microphone, and passes them on to the skull bones. You can understand how these hearing aids work by pressing one end of a rubber band hard against the bone you can feel just behind the ear. Stretch the band out and pluck it. You will hear the sound almost as loudly as when you held the band in your teeth.

HOW GOOD IS YOUR EAR?

Think of the variety of sounds in our world. Some are pleasant; some, like someone running his fingernails down a blackboard, are most unpleasant. Some sounds are very high and some are very, very low. Some you can hear, and some you can't! So now try The Lowest Sounds investigation. For *Things Needed* see page 79.

Loop the band around the box and pluck it. Be sure it makes a very low note. If you can pull the band around the box so that it is not stretched tightly over the opening, it will work even better. The band makes a very low sound because it is heavy, as you saw in A Musical Band. What happens if we make it heavier?

Fasten the paper clip to the middle of the band. Hold the clip and lift the band up with it. Let it go. You will see it vibrate and you may hear a very low note. If you hold the box you can feel the vibrations. If the band was very loose to begin with, you may find that you cannot hear any sound at all.

The Lowest Sounds

Things Needed:
"Fat" rubber band
Cardboard shoe box
Paper clip

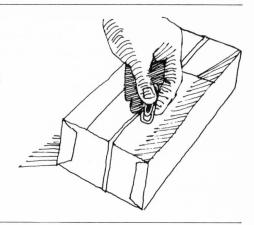

Everything that vibrates makes a sound. We cannot hear every sound, however. Some things vibrate too fast to be heard by people. Too fast is more than 20,000 times back and forth each second. Sounds that are above the range of our hearing are called *ultrasonic* sounds.

Things which vibrate too slowly are also impossible for us to hear. Too slow is less than 20 vibrations a second. These are *subsonic* sounds. We feel subsonic sounds, but we do not really hear them. Most young people can usually hear sounds between 20 and 20,000 vibrations a second. As people grow older, this range of hearing usually becomes smaller.

If you heard a sound when you plucked the paper clip weighted band, try making the band looser or find a fatter band. With a little experimenting you should be able to make the band vibrate less than 20 times a second, and make a subsonic sound.

You might be tempted to try to make a note with more than 20,000 vibrations a second by stretching the band very tight, but don't try. You would find that the band will not stretch tight enough; it will break well before it makes a sound above your upper range of hearing.

6

Final Fun-damentals

This final chapter is not really the end of the book. There are still many science mysteries that you can investigate using a rubber band. This chapter contains a collection of odd ones to get you started.

WHERE'S THE LOOP?

Here's a game you might play with a friend who claims to be a good observer:

Finding the Loop

Things Needed:
Fat rubber band, more than $3\frac{1}{2}$ inches long
Paper clip, straightened into a long wire

ODD NUMBER OF LAYERS (5)

EVEN NUMBER OF LAYERS (6)

Roll the band up from one end, along the flat side. You will notice that you have a roll which has two loops in the middle. The opening in one of these loops is inside the band, and the other is outside.

Ask your friend to put the paper clip through the hole he thinks is on the inside.

When he has made his choice let the band go. If he has chosen the proper loop the band will be caught on the clip. If it is the wrong one, the band will fall to the floor. Let him try it several times. Unless he is very clever, he will probably miss as often as he succeeds.

Surprisingly, this is actually a mathematical trick. You can choose the correct loop every time simply by counting.

Counting outward from the loops to the outside of the coil, you will find there is an even number of rubber-band layers on one side, and an odd number on the other. If you choose the loop with the odd number of rubber layers beside it, you will always be inside the band. You can also miss every time simply by choosing the loop with the even number of layers beside it.

It does not matter how long the band is, or how many times it coils around; this rule will always hold true. Call it the "Odd Rule" and you will remember which loop to choose to find the inside of the band.

SINGING STRINGS

Have you ever heard telephone wires sing? Sometimes when the wind is blowing, telephone and electric wires start to whistle and sigh very loudly. If you are alone, and it's getting on toward dark, this can be a very frightening sound.   It may even be responsible for more than one ghost story.   But what you hear are not the moans and groans of some sad spirit; they're good old-fashioned *aeolian sounds*.

Making Aeolian Sounds

Things Needed:
Four rubber bands,
    each about $3\frac{1}{2}$ inches long
Six paper clips

Loop the bands together to form a chain.   Hook all six paper clips on one end.   Hold the other end in your hand, and spin the bands around as fast as you can. When you are doing it properly, you will hear a shrill whistle.

Any wire, string, or rubber band will vibrate when the wind blows over it if it is stretched tightly enough. When you swing the rubber-band chain, the weight of the paper clips makes it stretch out.   And, instead of waiting for the wind to blow, you create your own by swinging the bands: the air itself is still, but it is moving across the bands.

But how does this motion become a sound-producing vibration?   Just as a ship, cutting through the water, creates *eddy currents* of swirling water behind it, the band creates eddy currents of air.   These tiny irregular swirls of air cause the band to move back and forth. As the wind gets stronger, the band moves more rapidly. Finally it is set into a strong vibration. The vibrating band then produces sound waves that your ear can hear.

Perhaps you can make different sounds, with the same band, by twirling it faster or slower. At different speeds it will vibrate in different ways, and cause different sounds.

These "old-fashioned" aeolian sounds were better known in your grandmother's time than they are today. Years ago people enjoyed *aeolian harps* or *wind harps*. These unusual string instruments were hung outdoors or in a screened porch. Every time the wind blew they made music.

You probably won't be able to find an aeolian harp today; even the clerk in a music shop might look at you oddly if you asked for one. But if you want to know whether that eerie music is really enjoyable, you can try making your own. For *Things Needed* see page 85.

Nail the pieces of wood together to make a rectangular frame. Be sure that it is firmly nailed.

Cut one band to make a long strip of rubber. Fasten one end of the band to the short end of the frame with a nail. Drive a nail in the opposite end of the frame, stretch the band as tightly as possible, and fasten it to the nail. Pound the nail in to hold the band.

The next time the wind blows hard, take the frame outdoors and hang it from a tree with a piece of string. If it works properly you will hear an occasional whistle. If it does not work, the band is probably not tight enough.

An Aeolian Harp

Things Needed:
Four rubber bands (different sizes)
Two pieces of wood, one foot long
Two pieces of wood, two feet long
Hammer
Nails
Piece of string about one foot long

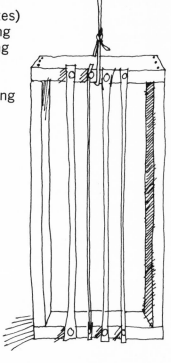

Once you have succeeded, and have found a nice windy spot for your harp, you might try to make it even more musical. The frame is wide enough for several more bands. Add the other bands, fastening them in place the same way you did the first. Be sure to try fatter and thinner bands. You will probably discover that some work better than others, and you will surely discover that they all make different sounds.

THE WONDERFUL RUBBER BAND THINGS

What are curved lines? Are they simply lines that are not straight?

Here is a curved line:

And, here is a smaller part of the same curve:

And, here is an even smaller part:

And, one still smaller:

This last one looks like a straight line. In fact, one way of thinking of curved lines is that they are made of many tiny straight lines, each one sloping just a bit more. Of course this is just one way to think about curves; another might be to think of them as a lot of tiny dots, like marbles, placed end to end, with each at a different angle from the previous one.

If you consider curves as being a great many straight lines, it is easy to put many straight lines together to make something that looks like a curve:

A Simple Rubber Band Thing

Things Needed:
Nine long rubber bands
Piece of heavy cardboard 5″ × 5″
Twelve-inch ruler
Pencil

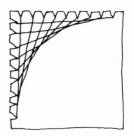

Make marks every half inch along the left and top edges of the cardboard square. Cut a notch at every mark. Loop a band around the cardboard, resting the band in the bottom notch at the left and the left-hand notch at the top. The next band goes in the notch above the first band on the left side, and to the right of the band at the top. Continue to loop bands in this way until all of the notches are filled. You will find that you have produced a graceful curve from rubber bands that are stretched perfectly straight!

By cutting more notches, and using more bands, you should be able to create even more beautiful curves, and perhaps even a circle.

A Complicated Rubber Band Thing

Things Needed:
Piece of heavy cardboard 5″ × 5″
Twelve-inch ruler
At least 36 rubber bands
Pencil

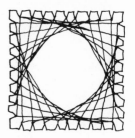

To begin, make marks every half inch along each edge of the cardboard. Cut a notch at every mark. Follow the directions for looping bands as described in A Simple Rubber Band Thing, but continue until you have rubber bands filling every notch on every edge. When you are finished, every notch will have two bands looped through it. The illustration will help you in arranging the bands. If you wish to make a still more complicated design, try adding more notches and more bands.

In these investigations you have created curves by carefully adding pieces of straight lines. Laying one over another resulted in an arc. Once you have made one curve this way you probably won't want to take it apart to show your friends how to do it. Perhaps you will want to make another Rubber Band Thing that will cross and uncross the bands to make, or unmake curves any number of times you wish.

Rubber Band Thing with a Twist

Things Needed:
Eight long rubber bands
Two 3$\frac{1}{2}$-inch heavy cardboard circles
Ruler
Pencil

First you must mark off the cardboard circles into sixteen even divisions around the edges. An easy way to do this is to cut a 3$\frac{1}{2}$-inch circle from paper, fold it in half, and then in half again. Continue folding it in half until you have folded it four times. When you open it out, it will have sixteen creases. Use these creases to show you where to mark the cardboard circles.

Cut a slot in each one of these marks. The slots should be one-quarter of an inch deep, starting from the edge of the circle. Now loop the bands around the two cardboard circles as shown. Each band should pass through two slots on each cardboard circle.

To operate your Rubber Band Thing with a Twist, hold one cardboard circle in each hand, and stretch the bands out. With all of the bands forming parallel lines between the disks, your Rubber Band Thing with a Twist will look something like a bird cage. Now, twist the cardboard ends of the cage and you will find that a beautiful curve appears. The graceful curves on the sides of the cage are called, mathematically, *hyperbolas*. This is the same kind of curve you can see on a wall close to a desk or floor lamp. The lampshade cuts off some of the light and the light that does strike the wall is in the shape of a hyperbola.

The hyperbola belongs to a very special group of mathematical figures. It is one of the least complicated shapes that a line can take. The other members of this group are the *straight line*, the *circle*, the *ellipse*, and the *parabola*.

You can see all of these shapes using your Rubber Band Thing with a Twist. The straight line is the stretched bands. The circle is one of the cardboard ends. The ellipse can be made by holding the bands parallel and pulling the cardboard ends slightly beside each other. If you imagine a line running around the center of the bands this would be an ellipse. And the easiest way to see a parabola might be to throw the Rubber Band Thing with a Twist away from you, slightly up in the air. The imaginary curve it would draw in the air during its upward and downward flight would be a parabola.

One final, more complicated, geometrical shape you can find with your Rubber Band Thing with a Twist is a *cone*. In fact, you can make two of them at the same time. Just twist the ends until the bands twist around each other at the middle. You will then be making two tiny "ice cream cones" with their points touching.

SOME QUESTIONS TO TRY

Finally, here are some things you might enjoy investigating on your own. Some may lead you to further books to find answers. Some you might already know. All of them will remind you that there are still many more investigations that can be made with the simple little things called rubber bands.

1. Make two marks one inch apart on a rubber band. Place the band on a ruler and stretch it to twice its length. How far apart will your marks be? What if you stretch the band to three times its length?
2. Can a rubber band be used to erase pencil marks?
3. Make a hill from some books and a piece of board. Tie a rubber band on the front bumper of a model car. Pull the car up the hill by tugging on the band. Now, lift the car off the ground by holding the band. Which method, lifting or tugging, is the easier way to move the car up?
4. Which is stronger, a rubber band or a piece of string? Devise a method of hanging books on each one. Add more books until they break. Which one can support the most books? Can you think of a reason why?
5. If you throw a rubber band, as hard as you can, at a sheet of writing paper, nothing will happen. But, if you snap the band toward the same paper you can easily make a hole in it. Where does the band get its extra "muscle" when you snap it?
6. How many times its length can you stretch a rubber band before it breaks? A one-inch band has been

stretched ten inches, which is ten times its length. Can you beat this?

7. Tie a knot in the center of a thin rubber band. Place one loop of the band across one open end of a five-inch section of plastic drinking straw, stretch the band along the straw, and place the other loop across the opposite end. Put the straw on a table. Now, with scissors, snip the band on one side of the knot. The straw will shoot, like an arrow, away from the scissors. Does the rubber band move at the same time? If so, which way? Why?

8. There is an easy way that a rubber band can be used to draw a circle. Can you think of it? A hint: Besides the band and a pencil, you will probably need a thumbtack.

9. Good luck with rubber band investigations of your own.

Index

ABOUT THE AUTHOR

Laurence B. White, Jr. may well be the world's only serious rubber-band collector: in the course of preparing this book he amassed about 500 specimens in assorted sizes, shapes, and colors. But collecting, and his membership in the Society of American Magicians, are only parts of his major interest, which is the dramatic presentation of scientific ideas. As Assistant Director of the Needham (Massachusetts) Science Center and as a popular television teacher he has ample opportunities to employ his unique talents. A native of Massachusetts, Mr. White now lives in Stoughton with his wife and two sons.